Games, Games, More Games!

101 great ideas for youth clubs

DayOne

© Day One Publications 2009

First printed 2009

ISBN 978-1-84625-168-9

British Library Cataloguing in Publication Data available

Published by Day One Publications

Ryelands Road, Leominster, England, HR6 8NZ

Telephone 01568 613 740   FAX 01568 611 473

email—sales@dayone.co.uk

web site—www.dayone.co.uk

North American e-mail—usasales@dayone.co.uk

North American web site—www.dayonebookstore.com

Printed by Gutenberg Press, Malta

Dedication

To my parents,
with gratitude for their
faithful Christian parenting

Endorsements

We all know of games for children and young people as we played them when we were their age and enjoyed most, if not all, of them—whether at home, school, clubs or camps. So why is it that, if you are like me, when we have to plan an event with games in, we can't think of anything suitable?

This little book is worth its weight in gold as it provides a ready collection of games we know, or even don't know, for us to dip into and use freely. Tirzah has compiled this useful resource for all who work with children and young people. For this, I am most grateful to her, and so will many others be! It is a resource that all who work with children and young people will find invaluable and great fun for the groups they work with.

Gareth James
Minister in Barton-upon-Humber, UK, and former youth pastor

Youth workers are very often not all-rounders! This book is a brilliant resource for someone like me—I always get stuck when it comes to planning games. For variety, simplicity and the fun factor, this book is what you need.

Sheila Stephen
Lecturer in Youth & Children's Ministry, Wales Evangelical School of Theology

Contents

Preface

Do you ever find yourself planning your youth work and struggling to think of games? There are often plenty of resources with ideas for crafts, activities and talks, but what about those times when all you want are some games ideas?

I have been involved in youth work all my life. Growing up in a minister's family, I have been an observer and participant in youth work from birth, and for the past fourteen years I have been involved in Sunday school, youth groups, camps, church weekends, and so on. I am currently a full-time youth worker and have discovered that there is a great lack of books that you can just pick up to find a suitable game. This book is an attempt to fill that gap, containing games that are suitable for a variety of ages and contexts.

I am not certain of the origin of many of these games; you may recognize some of them under other names or with slightly different rules. I have picked them up over the years of doing youth work. Some I was taught as a child and have been around for years; others I have learned from fellow youth workers.

To help you find something appropriate for your group, the games are grouped into the following categories:

- Gap-fillers—five-minute games
- Action time—active games
- Mind-benders—thinking games
- Easy-going games—non-active games

Within each category, games are organized according to the age group for which they are best suited. Games suitable for all ages come first, followed by games for:

- Infants: 4–7 years
- Juniors: 8–11 years
- Secondary: 12+ years.

A symbol shows whether the game is suitable for playing indoors or outdoors, or both.

 Outdoors  Indoors

If you are using these games in a church youth group or as part of a Holiday Bible Club, you may like to adapt them to illustrate a particular point or to fit in with your theme. Below are some suggestions as to how this can be done with some of the games; with a little imagination, most of the games can be adapted to help make a more streamlined session.

Fishes in the sea
Instead of using fish, you could base this game around farm animals and a farmer.

Mummy!
If you are covering the story of Lazarus, you could use this game to illustrate Lazarus emerging from his grave clothes.

Pictionary

You could choose items from the story you are about to tell (or have just told) as a way to introduce or reinforce it; for example, if you are covering the story of David and Goliath, you could choose 'giant', 'sling', 'stones', etc.

Directions

Without someone to direct us, we are lost, and without God/the Bible we are spiritually lost. This game is good for discussing spiritual blindness.

Mr Noah

This game can be adapted and used to tell virtually any story in the Bible. It is sometimes a good way to introduce a story before applying it.

Captain's coming

This can be a great game if your story is about Jonah, or Paul shipwrecked, etc., as it gets people thinking topically.

Crows and cranes

This can be changed very simply to fit in with any theme; for example, if you are talking about Moses, you could use 'manna' and 'quail', helping to get certain terms fixed in your players' minds.

Hunt the leader

You could get all your leaders to dress as characters from a Bible story.

Categories game

The categories can be changed to fit many different themes and stories, depending on the particular point you wish to emphasize.

Book hold

When a player's arms grow weary, you could get a friend to help by holding up the player's hands and use this to introduce Exodus 17:8–16 and Israel defeating the Amalekites.

I hope you find this a useful addition to your youth-work resources.

Tirzah L. Jones

Note

All leaders should check the child protection policies of their church or organization before running these games and ensure that they follow the requirements laid out in them.

Gap-fillers

1 Simon says

What you need

Age range

All ages

How to play

1. Give the group simple commands, such as 'Jump up and down', 'Stand on one leg', etc.

2. The group must obey these commands only if you say 'Simon says ...' first (e.g., 'Simon says jump up and down').

3. If you omit 'Simon says', the group should ignore the command.

4. Each player has three lives. Any player who performs a wrong command loses a life.

5. When players have lost all three lives, they are out.

6. Once players begin to understand the game, they can take it in turns to give the commands.

Variation:
Change the level of instructions to fit your age group; for older players, use more elaborate instructions.

2 Scrambled word puzzles

What you need

- 1 list of scrambled words per team (e.g., 'uhflitfa' for 'faithful')
- 1 pen per team

Age range

All ages

How to play

1. Divide everyone into teams of four.

2. Give each team a list of the scrambled words.

3. Start all the teams at the same time. The aim is to find all the hidden words.

4. The winning team is the one that finishes first or has most correct solutions within a certain time limit.

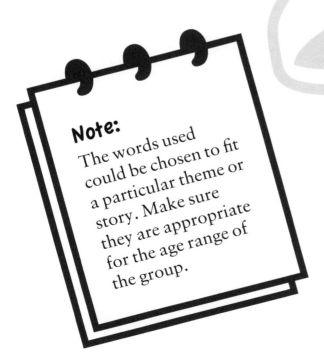

Note:
The words used could be chosen to fit a particular theme or story. Make sure they are appropriate for the age range of the group.

3 Guess what I am

What you need

Age range

All ages

How to play

1. The first player must think of a person, place or a thing.

2. This player must then tell the group whether he or she is a person, place or thing.

3. The other players then ask questions (e.g., Are you blue? Can you speak? Do you bark? Can you be eaten? Are you alive? Are you in this country?) until they guess who/what/where the person is.

4. The person who guesses correctly goes next, and so on.

4 Place your team in order

What you need

Age range

All ages

How to play

1. Split players into two teams.

2. Get all the players in each team to form a chain by holding hands.

3. Shout an instruction to the teams; they must follow the instruction without breaking their chain.

4. The winning team is the one that completes the task fastest.

5. Suggestions for how to play:

   by age order
   by height order
   boys first, then girls
   by the month they were born in
   group according to hair colour
   group according to eye colour
   group according to those with long
   or short sleeves, etc.

5 Pushing the matchbox

What you need

- 1 party blowout per player (the type that unrolls like a tongue when you blow it)
- 1 matchbox per player

Age range

All ages

How to play

1. Each player has a matchbox and a party blowout. Using the party blowout, players have to push their matchbox to the finishing line.

2. Players may not touch the matchbox with anything other than the tongue of the party blowout!

Note: This can be played in heats or everyone together.

6 Memory game

What you need
- 12 random objects
- 1 tray
- Paper
- Pens

Age range
All ages

How to play
1. Lay out all twelve items on the tray.

2. Give everyone three minutes to memorize all the items on the tray. Then remove the tray or cover it up.

3. Hand out pens and paper and give players a further three minutes to write down as many objects on the tray as they can.

Note:
This can be played in teams or individually.

7 Sleeping lions

What you need

Age range

Infants

How to play

1. Get all the players to lie down on their backs.

2. Walk around and try to make the players blink, move, smile, etc.

3. Whenever a player makes any kind of movement, he or she is removed from the game.

4. The winner is the player still lying on the floor at the end.

Note: This game is perfect for quietening everyone down.

8 Spy and rhyme

What you need

Age range

Juniors/secondary

How to play

1. This game is similar to 'I Spy'.

2. One player is to be chosen as 'It'.

3. 'It' thinks of a word, then gives a clue by saying a word that it rhymes with. For example: 'This is a word that rhymes with "spoon" and can be found at night' (answer: 'moon').

4. The player who guesses the correct answer is 'It' next.

9 Yes/no

What you need

Age range

Juniors/secondary

How to play

1. Seat one player in the centre of the room.

2. Ask this player a series of questions. He or she must answer without using the words 'yes' or 'no'.

3. The aim is to try to catch the player out.

10 Human knot

What you need

Age range

Juniors/secondary

How to play

1. Get all the players to stand in a circle with their hands out in front of them.

2. Players should then take hold of different people's hands.

3. Every player should be holding hands with other players; there should be no breaks.

4. Now tell players to unknot themselves into a circle without letting go of anyone's hand.

11 Hula-hoop pass

What you need

- 1 hula hoop

Age range

Juniors/secondary

How to play

1. Everyone stands in a circle holding hands.

2. Place the hula hoop over one pair of hands.

3. The object of the game is to pass the hula hoop all the way round the circle without anyone letting go of anybody's hand.

12 Rhythm 1 to 2

What you need

Age range
Secondary

How to play

1. Give everyone a number and seat them in a circle.

2. Get all the players to tap their thighs then clap their hands in rhythm (slow beat).

3. In time with the clapping, the first person says, for example, 'Number 1 to number 12' (i.e. his or her number to someone else's number).

4. Keeping the rhythm, the person whose number was called then says, 'Number … to number …', and so on. The idea is to increase the speed and catch someone out.

5. If a person doesn't respond when his or her number is called, or if someone calls a wrong number, he or she is out (that person must stay in the circle and continue with the rhythm clapping, but if another player then calls that person's number again, that player is also out).

6. The game gets faster and faster. To stay in the game, players need to remember who is out and concentrate on the numbers being called.

Action time

13 Directions

What you need
- 2 blindfolds
- 2 chairs

Age range
All ages

How to play
1. Split the group into two teams.

2. Select one member from each team.

3. Blindfold these two players, then place two chairs in different places in the room. Assign one chair to each team.

4. Each team must direct its blindfolded player to its chair through shouted instructions, e.g., 'Go left', 'Forward a bit', 'Turn around', etc.

5. Both teams shout out instructions at the same time, aiming to disorientate the other team's blindfolded player while getting their player to their chair fastest.

14 Crows and cranes

ᴴᴛᴛᴴ

What you need

Age range
All ages

How to play

1. Each person chooses a partner.

2. Place all players in two rows, each player facing his or her partner.

3. Name one row 'cranes' and the other, 'crows'.

4. The crows should stand on one side of the room and the cranes on the other; leave a gap between the players and the wall.

5. If you shout 'Crows', the crows must cross to the opposite wall without being touched by the cranes, and vice versa.

6. Add confusion by shouting random words that sound like 'crow' or 'crane'.

7. Points are awarded to the team that has been most successful either in escaping capture or in capturing members of the opposite team.

15 Clumps

What you need

Age range
All ages

How to play

1. Gather all the players into the centre of the room.

2. The leader must think of a category; for example, 'Blue eyes'.

3. All players with blue eyes then form into a group.

4. Any players who do not fit into the category or who are too slow are out.

5. The aim is to end up with one player left.

6. Other categories could include 'three' (players must form into groups of three; any left over are out); 'players with a sister'; 'players wearing red'; etc.

Variation:
Change the level of instructions to fit the age of your group; for older players, use more elaborate instructions.

16 Scavenger hunt

What you need

Each team needs:

- List of items to scavenge (about 20)
- 1 carrier bag

Age range

All ages

How to play

1. Split into groups of three or four.

2. Give each group the list of items.

3. Teams must then scatter to find all the items on the list and place them in the carrier bag.

4. Once all the items have been collected, the teams return.

5. Scoring: the first team back gets 10 bonus points. Each correct item gets 1 point.

6. The winning team is the team with the most points.

Note:
This game is good for the beach/woods etc.

17 Mr Noah

What you need

- Chairs

Age range

All ages

How to play

1. Seat all the players in rows with two players per row, facing the same direction and an arm's width apart.

2. Call the first row 'Mr Noah'; the second, 'Noah's wife'; the next three rows, Noah's sons 'Ham', 'Shem' and 'Japheth'; all the other rows an animal name.

3. Tell the story of Noah. When you mention Noah's wife, for example, those on the row named 'Noah's wife' must get up, run round the outside to the front of the rows and then up the middle and back to their seats. This is repeated every time you mention the name of one of the rows in the story.

4. Don't pause in the telling of the story. Sometimes you will have more than one row running at a time.

5. If you say 'all the family', everyone named 'Noah', 'Mrs Noah', 'Ham', 'Shem' or 'Japheth' must run.

6. If you say 'all the animals', everyone with an animal name runs.

7. If you say 'the ark', all the players must run.

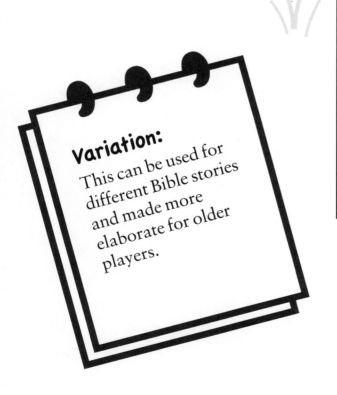

Variation:
This can be used for different Bible stories and made more elaborate for older players.

18 Back and forth

What you need
- Space markers, e.g., cones

Age range
All ages

How to play

1. Mark out four bases. Split the group into teams.

2. The first team member runs to 1st base, then back to start, then to 2nd base and back to start, then to 3rd base and back to start, then to 4th base and back to start.

3. That player then takes the second player by the hand and together they repeat the exercise.

4. Then the third player joins the line, and so on until all team members are in the line

5. The fastest team to complete the race wins.

Variation:
You can use jumpers, shoes, etc. to mark the bases.

19 Captain's coming

What you need

Age range

All ages

Variation:
Change the level of instructions to fit your group; for older players, use more elaborate instructions.

How to play

1. Name each part of the room as follows:

   Left-hand side: Port
   Right-hand side: Starboard
   Front: Bow
   Back: Fore
   Centre: Midships

2. Give commands, such as 'Port': players must then run to that particular place. The last one to reach the destination is out.

3. Other commands include:

   Man overboard: players dive on the floor
   Lifeboats: players get into two groups and row
   Climb the rigging: players climb on the spot
   Shark in the water: players act like sharks
   Scrub the deck: players kneel on the floor scrubbing
   Captain's coming: players must line up in the centre of the room in silence and salute the leader

4. Keep going until only one player is left.

5. You can confuse players by saying, e.g., 'Port' when they are already there; any who move are then out.

20 Shooting hoops

What you need

- 1 hoop
- 1 ball

Age range

All ages

How to play

1. Divide up the group into teams.

2. Each player gets one chance to land the ball within the hoop.

3. Count the number of successful throws. The team with the most in five minutes wins.

21 Dribble

What you need

- Space markers
- 1 football
- 2 goals, or goal markers

Age range

All ages

How to play

1. Split the group into two teams.

2. Line up the players, one behind the other in their teams, in front of the space markers.

3. Each team supplies a goalie.

4. The players must dribble the ball around all the space markers and then try to shoot a goal. The goalie has to try to save the shot.

5. If the player does not go round all the space markers, he or she must go back to the beginning.

6. All team members must have a go.

7. Scoring: 1 point for every goal scored. If the goalie makes a save, the goalie's team gets a point.

22 Under and over

What you need

- 2 balls

Age range

All ages

How to play

1. Split the group into two teams and line up the teams side by side.

2. Each team has to pass a ball from the person at the front to the person at the back.

3. The first player in each team has to pass the ball overhead; the second passes under his or her legs; the third passes overhead, and so on.

4. When the ball reaches the back of the line, the player at the back runs to the front and starts it again. The game continues until that last player is back at the end of the line again. When a team has finished, everyone in the team must sit down.

5. The winning team is the first to finish and be sitting down.

23 Sopping sponge

What you need

- 1 sponge for each team
- 2 buckets for each team
- Water
- 1 measuring jug

Age range

All ages

How to play

1. Divide everyone into teams and stand them in lines.

2. At the head of each line, place a sponge and a bucket containing water. At the back of each line, place an empty bucket to collect water.

3. When the leader shouts 'Go!', the person at the front of each line dips the sponge into the water and passes it to the back of the line, where the last person squeezes the water into the bucket.

4. The person at the back then runs to the front with the sponge and begins again.

5. When all the players are back in their original places, the team sits down to indicate that they have finished.

6. The team that manages to collect the most water wins.

Note:
Be prepared for wet players and floors!

24 Wellie throw

What you need

- 1 Wellington or other boot
- 1 line marker
- 1 other marker (e.g., a shoe or anything else to hand)

Age range

All ages

How to play

1. Line the players up behind the line marker.

2. Give the first player the boot. He or she must throw it as far as possible. Mark where it lands.

3. Each player gets to throw the boot. Only mark the furthest throws.

4. The player who throws the furthest wins.

Variation:
This can be played individually or with teams.

25 Talent contest

What you need

Age range
All ages

How to play

1. Advance notice needs to be given to the group.

2. Each person turns up ready to perform his or her particular talent to the rest of the group.

   Talents may include joke-telling, playing musical instruments, skipping, football skills, etc.

26 Football skills

What you need

- Net
- 1 football
- Space markers

Age range

All ages

How to play

1. Split the group into two teams.

2. Each team must complete each of the following football skills within a set time limit.

   dribbling
   passing
   shooting

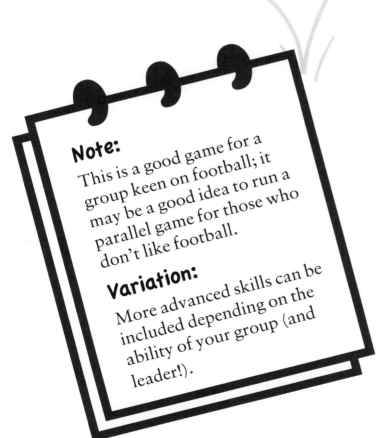

Note:

This is a good game for a group keen on football; it may be a good idea to run a parallel game for those who don't like football.

Variation:

More advanced skills can be included depending on the ability of your group (and leader!).

27 Apple bobbing

What you need

- 2 bowls of water
- 1 apple per player

Age range

All ages

How to play

1. Split the players into two teams.

2. Place an apple in each bowl of water.

3. Players from each team must take it in turns to run forward and get their apple out of the bowl without using their hands.

4. The team that finishes the quickest wins.

Note:
Use fresh water and a different apple for each player. If playing indoors, be prepared for wet floors!

28 Ambiguous scavenger hunt

What you need

- 1 plastic bag per team
- List of items per team

Age range

All ages

How to play

1. Split the players into teams of three or four.

2. Give each team a list of non-specific items to find (see examples below).

3. The team with the most original ideas wins.

4. The following could go on the list:

   something old
   something new
   something blunt
   something green
   something useful
   something pretty
   something ugly
   something educational
   something useless
   something electronic

29 500 up for grabs

What you need

- 1 large soft ball

Age range

All ages

How to play

1. One player is the thrower. All the other players stand around the thrower.

2. The thrower throws the ball into the air and shouts a number between 50 and 500.

3. The other players have to try to catch the ball before it touches the floor. Whoever catches it gets the number of points that the thrower shouted.

4. If a player drops the ball, he or she loses that number of points.

5. The thrower stays the same throughout the game. The first player to get 500 points wins and becomes the next thrower.

30 Capture the flag

What you need

- 2 flags (or anything that could represent a flag, e.g., a brightly coloured top)
- Ideally a room/field with lots of places to hide (e.g., hidey holes or bushes)

Age range

All ages

How to play

1. Split the room/field into two territories. Mark out an area as the 'jail'.

2. Split the players into two teams and give each team a flag.

3. Give each team five minutes to hide its flag.

4. When the time is up, each team has to capture the opposing team's flag.

5. Anyone who is caught must go to jail and can only be freed when a team member grabs him or her when no one else is looking.

6. The first team to get the opposing team's flag into its territory wins.

Variation:
While the flag is being hidden, spies can be sent out to see where the flag is hidden, and look-outs can be sent out to spot the spies.

31 Hotter– colder

What you need

• An item to hide

Age range

All ages

How to play

1. One player leaves the room.

2. While he or she is gone, the object is hidden.

3. When the player returns, he or she has to find the hidden item.

4. Everyone else shouts out comments depending on how close the player is to the hidden item:

   warmer, hotter, burning, etc. if the player is close
   cold, tepid, freezing, etc. if the player is nowhere near the item

32 Indoor netball

What you need

- 1 ball
- 2 containers of the same size and that are big enough to hold the ball
- 2 chairs

Age range

All ages

How to play

1. Divide the players into two teams. Place two chairs at opposite ends of the room. These are the 'nets'.

2. One player on each team volunteers to be goalie and is given a container. They stand on the chairs.

3. Play starts from the centre. Team members must try to score by throwing the ball into the container manned by the opposing team's goalie.

4. The ball can only be passed by being thrown from one player to another.

5. There must be no running with the ball and no direct contact with other players.

6. The ball must pass to three people before a goal can be scored.

7. The ball must be thrown, not placed, into the container. The goalie must hold the container still when the opposing team is trying to score. Points will be deducted from the goalie's team if he or she tries to stop the other team from scoring.

Variation:
Adapt the rules to suit the age of the players.

33 Stay away

What you need

- 1 ball

Age range

All ages

How to play

1. Stand everyone in a large circle.

2. One player stands in the centre. He or she is 'It'.

3. Players must pass the ball around the circle in any direction without the player in the centre intercepting it.

4. If the player catches the ball, he or she changes places with the player who threw it last.

34 Empty chair!

What you need

• 1 chair per player

Age range

All ages

How to play

1. Everyone sits on chairs in a circle.

2. One player stands in the centre, leaving an empty chair in the circle.

3. The other players then move around so that the position of the empty chair keeps changing.

4. The player in the centre has to sit on the empty chair.

5. When this player finally manages to sit on the empty chair, the last person to find a chair goes in the centre, and so on.

35 Ice-cube hunt

What you need

- 1 tray of ice cubes per team
- 1 bucket
- 1 measuring jug

Age range

All ages

How to play

1. Divide the players into teams.

2. Give each team a bucket. Place the tray of ice cubes in front of each team but a good distance away.

3. Each team has to collect and carry all its ice cubes back to the bucket, one at a time, before they melt. They can only carry them using their hands.

4. Measure at the end how much water is in each team's bucket. The team with the most water wins.

36 Pop-bottle skittles

What you need

- 10 large fizzy-drinks bottles, half-filled with water and with the lids securely tightened
- 1 beanbag

Age range

All ages

How to play

1. Arrange the bottles in the same way as skittles: four at the back, three in front of them, two in front of them, then one at the very front.

2. The players must stand at a distance from the bottles. Using a beanbag, they must knock over as many bottles as possible, with points being gained for the number they knock over.

37 Hole in the bucket

What you need

- 2 buckets per team, 1 of them filled with water
- 1 tin can per team with holes punched in it (make sure there are no sharp edges on the tin can)
- 1 measuring jug

Age range

All ages

How to play

1. Divide the players into teams.

2. Team members must take it in turns to run forward to the bucket filled with water, dip in the can and fill it with water, balance the can on their heads and run back to their team, pouring the water that is left into the empty bucket.

3. Points are awarded for finishing first and for the amount of water collected in the bucket.

Note:
Be prepared for wet players!

38 Islands

What you need
- Newspaper

Age range
All ages

How to play
1. Scatter the newspaper on the floor around the room.

2. Play some music; everyone must walk around the room without touching the newspaper pieces.

3. Stop the music. As soon as this happens, players must jump onto the newspaper; several players can be on each piece of newspaper.

4. Any player not on some newspaper is out.

5. As the game proceeds, remove some newspaper and rip some up to make the islands smaller.

39 Dodge ball

What you need

- 1 soft ball

Age range

All ages

How to play

1. One or two players become the 'taggers'; they have to tag the other players by hitting them below the knee with the ball.

2. Any player that gets tagged sits out.

Variation:
There are lots of variation to this basic game which you can invent. It can be played as teams or as individuals.

40 Sack race

What you need

- 1 sack per team

Age range

All ages

How to play

1. Divide the players into teams.

2. Players in each team take it in turns to jump in the sack to the end of the room and back again.

3. Once everyone in the team has run, the team sits down to indicate that it has finished.

41 Mice tails

What you need

- String

Age range

Infants

How to play

1. Cut up enough string for each player to have one piece each.

2. Tuck the string into the back of each player's trousers.

3. When you shout 'Go!', all the players must run around and take as many pieces of string as possible from the others while protecting their own.

4. The game ends when everyone's string has been taken.

5. The winner is the one with the most pieces of string at the end.

42 What's the time, Mr Wolf?

What you need

Age range

Infants

How to play

1. One player is chosen to be Mr Wolf.

2. Mr Wolf stands away from everybody else with his back turned to them. He must not turn around.

3. The other players stand in a line behind him and call out, 'What's the time, Mr Wolf?'

4. Mr Wolf answers with a time. If, for example, he says '2 o'clock', the other players move forward two paces; if he says '5 o'clock', they move forward five paces.

5. The players keep asking and keep moving forward.

6. Whenever he chooses, Mr Wolf can shout 'Dinner time!', and can then quickly turn around and try to catch somebody. The other players have to try to run away before they are caught.

43 Egg and spoon race

What you need

- 1 spoon per team
- Eggs (raw or hardboiled, depending on how messy you want to be)

Age range

Infants/juniors

How to play

1. Divide the players into teams.

2. Players from each team take it in turns to balance the egg on the spoon and, without dropping the egg, run to the end of the room and back to their team.

3. After every player in the team has run, the team sits down. The team that sits down first wins.

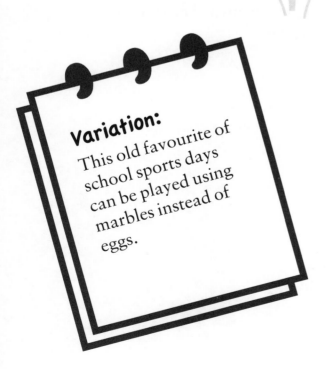

Variation:
This old favourite of school sports days can be played using marbles instead of eggs.

44 Queenie

What you need

- 1 ball

Age range

Infants/juniors

How to play

1. A player is picked to be 'Queenie'. Queenie turns his or her back to everyone else and throws the ball over his or her shoulder. One of the other players must catch or pick up the ball.

2. All the players except Queenie put their hands behind their backs so that Queenie won't know who has the ball.

3. Queenie then turns around and everyone shouts, 'Queenie, Queenie, who's got the ball?'

4. By a process of elimination, Queenie has to guess who has the ball.

5. If the person with the ball is last to be picked, that person is the new Queenie.

45 Animal noises

What you need

Age range

Infants/juniors

How to play

1. Think of four animals. Call all the players forward one at a time and assign to them one of the animals by whispering into their ears.

2. When everyone has been assigned an animal, shout 'Go!' All the players have to make the noise of the animal they've been given.

3. The players have to locate everyone else assigned to their particular animal, e.g., cats have to find all the other cats. They can only do this through making their animal noises.

4. Players should then group together according to animal type.

46 Fishes in the sea

What you need

Age range

Infants/juniors

Note: This is particularly good with younger children.

How to play

1. Seat all the players on chairs in a circle.

2. Choose the names of three fish and give each player one of these names.

3. Begin to tell a story like this: 'One day, the shark went out for a swim' (all those named 'shark' start walking around the edge of the circle). Continue the story in the same way, ending up by shouting, 'The fishermen are out!' At this, all the players must run back to their seats.

4. While you tell the story, remove a chair; the player without a chair to sit on at the end is out.

5. Other instructions could include:

   'Tide turned': walk the opposite way round the circle
   'Sea got rough': walk fast
   'Sea was calm': walk slowly
   or call out more than one fish name at a time

47 Statues

What you need

Age range
Infants/juniors

How to play

1. Get all the players walking around slowly.

2. Call out an instruction, such as:

   ballerina
   someone scoring a goal
   sleeping cat
   tiger
   Olympic racer
   archer
   driver in a car
   soldier
   teacher
   rugby player

3. All players must then make a statue of this. Give 1 point to the best statue.

Note:
This is particularly good with younger children

48 Dog and bone

What you need

- 1 beanbag

Age range

Infants/juniors

How to play

1. Split the players into two teams.

2. Number each team member. They are the 'dogs'.

3. Place the beanbag in the centre of the room. This is the 'bone'.

4. When a number is called, the dogs (one player from each team with that number) must run to the centre of the room and try to grab the bone (beanbag) and make it back to their seat without being caught by their opponent.

49 Duck, duck, goose

What you need

Age range

Infants/juniors

How to play

1. All the players sit in a circle.

2. Choose one player from the group.

3. He or she walks around the outside of the circle tapping each player on the head and saying 'Duck' with each tap.

4. The player must say 'Goose' on one occasion.

5. When the player says 'Goose', the person tapped must get up and chase the player round the circle and try to catch him or her.

6. The player being chased must run round the whole circle and sit in the other player's place. If caught, he or she is out.

7. The game continues in this way.

50 Spell your name

What you need

Age range

Juniors

How to play

1. Pick a player to be the leader.

2. This player stands with his or her back to the rest of the players, who stand about ten metres away.

3. The leader calls out a letter of the alphabet. Any player whose name contains that letter can move forward; the number of steps forward depends on the number of times that letter appears in the player's name.

4. The leader keeps calling out letters until someone reaches him or her.

51 Cabbage

What you need

- 1 large soft ball

Age range

Juniors/secondary

How to play

1. Give each player a number.

2. Stand in a circle and give one person the ball. He or she throws the ball in the air and quickly calls a random number. All the other players must run as far as possible from the ball, but the player whose number has been called must catch the ball and shout 'cabbage', and stand still. As soon as they hear the word 'cabbage', all the other players must stop moving.

3. The player with the ball stays standing still and throws it at another player.

4. If the player targeted is hit or moves, he or she is out. If the thrower misses, the thrower is out.

5. If the ball rolls and hits other players on the way to its target, all these players are out.

6. The ball is then given to whichever of the two (player or target) is not out.

7. Call all into the circle and start again.

8. If the caller calls the number of a player who is already out, the caller is also out.

9. Aim to end up with one player left, who is the winner.

52 Who, sir? Me, sir?

What you need

- 1 chair for every player

Age range

Juniors/secondary

How to play

1. Put the players into pairs.

2. Put the chairs in rows of two and get each pair to sit in a row (like sitting in a classroom).

3. Number the rows from 1 to …

4. You start off by saying something like, 'Yesterday I went to the beach, and on my way there someone stole my bucket and spade, and they were in row number 3.'

5. The pair in row 3 must stand up together and say, 'Who, sir? Me, sir? No, Sir, not I, sir, it was number … , sir.'

6. The player on the right-hand side chooses the row number and shouts it out, and the pair in the new row called get up and repeat the phrase, and so on.

7. If a pair are slow getting up or fail to speak together, they are sent to the back of the class.

8. Everyone else then moves forward one row to fill the space they have left.

9. The row numbers belong to the seats, so every time a pair move, they change row number.

53 Competition exercises

What you need

Age range
Juniors/secondary

How to play

1. Choose a selection of exercises.

2. Divide the group into teams.

3. Each player in each team must complete as many of the chosen exercises as possible in five minutes.

4. Each team adds up the total number completed.

5. The team with the highest score wins.

Variation:
Any form of exercise can be used, e.g., step-ups, press-ups, push-ups, etc.

54 Cross the square in ten

What you need
- 1 ball

Age range
Juniors/secondary

How to play

1. Divide up the players into two teams.

2. Mark out a large area (about the size of a football pitch or tennis court).

3. Line one team up on one side of the area and give them the ball. The team must then move from one side to the other, passing the ball to each other without dropping it (similar to rugby).

4. They must do this in two minutes and pass the ball exactly ten times (players may handle the ball more than once, but all the team must be used).

5. Players may not go outside the marked area; if they do, they are out.

6. A player may not move when holding the ball in his or her hand.

7. Other team members must not stand closer than arm's length from the player with the ball.

8. If the team is successful, a player of the opposition team is removed from the game.

9. If the team is unsuccessful, it loses one of its players.

10. The ball then passes to the other team, who must perform the same task.

11. The game goes on until only one team is left.

55 Catch ball

What you need

- 1 ball

Age range

Juniors/secondary

How to play

1. Get everyone to stand in a circle facing one another. One player has the ball.

2. The player throws the ball to someone in the circle after calling his or her name.

3. If the other player catches it, he or she must spin around once and then throw it to someone else after calling out his or her name, and so on.

4. If you drop the ball, you must place one hand behind your back.

5. If you catch the ball the next time, you may go back to using both hands to catch the ball.

6. If you drop the ball twice or more, you must first go down on one knee, then down on both knees, then sit down, then lie down. If you drop the ball when lying down, you are out of the game and must stay lying down until the end of the game.

7. The winner is the last person left not lying down.

56 Crazy rounders

What you need

- 1 rounders bat
- 1 rounders ball

Age range

Juniors/secondary

How to play

1. Choose one batsman and one bowler. All other players field.

2. The game is played like rounders. The ball is bowled underarm at the batsman. If he or she strikes the ball and hits it, he or she must turn anticlockwise on the spot to score a run. Each complete turn scores 1 run; the batsman can spin as many times as he or she wants.

3. As soon as the ball is returned to the bowler, the ball can be bowled again.

4. If the batsman fails to hit the ball, he or she must turn three times clockwise. Again, as soon as the ball is returned to the bowler, another ball may be bowled. If the player has not yet completed the three rotations, he or she cannot bat; the ball passes and the batsman is out. If the ball hit by the batsman is caught, he or she is also out.

57 Three tags and out

What you need

Age range

Juniors/secondary

How to play

1. Mark out a large square area; all the players must stay inside this area.

2. Choose one player whose job it is to tag as many people as possible.

3. The first time players are tagged, they must put one hand behind their back; the second time, they must put the other hand behind their back; the third time, they must hop with both hands behind their back.

4. The fourth time players are tagged, they are out.

58 Cross-the-room challenge

What you need

• Lots of pieces of paper

Age range

Juniors/secondary

How to play

1. Split the group into two teams.

2. Each team is given one fewer sheet of paper than the number of players in the team (e.g., five team members get four pieces of paper).

3. The teams start off at opposite sides of the room. The idea is to get all their team members to the other side of the room without standing on the floor.

4. If a team member touches the floor, all members of that team must return to the start.

5. The team that gets across first wins.

59 Egg throw

What you need

- 1 egg per pair

Age range

Juniors/secondary

How to play

1. Split the group into pairs. Form the pairs into two lines, with players facing their partners.

2. Give all the players in one of the lines an egg. These players must pass the eggs to their partners. Once they have done that, they must take one step backwards.

3. The partners must then, all together, pass the eggs back to the first players. The first players now take another step backwards and then, in unison, throw the eggs back to their partners; they then take another step back, the eggs are passed back to them, and so on.

4. The pair that gets the furthest apart without breaking the egg wins.

5. It is important that the eggs get passed at the same time and that all the players take the same-sized step backwards.

60 Team tag

What you need

Age range

Juniors/secondary

How to play

1. Mark out a large square area (needs to be about the size of a tennis court).

2. All the players stand within the square; no one may leave the square.

3. Nominate one player and shout 'Go!'

4. This player may run and touch anyone in the square, who then must hold his or her hand; the player then goes after someone else, and so on.

5. The chain of players will get longer and the number of free players will get smaller. No player can be tagged if the chain is broken.

6. The winner is the last player to be tagged.

61 Rugby dribble

What you need

- 2 rugby balls
- Set of space markers (clothes or shoes can be used if necessary)

Age range

Juniors/secondary

How to play

1. Split players into two teams.

2. Set out the space markers in the same way for each team.

3. Player 1 of each team dribbles the rugby ball around the course and back. Then player 2 does the same, etc.

4. The winning team is the one who can do the most runs in five minutes.

62 Chair lifecraft

What you need

- 1 chair per team member

Age range

Juniors/secondary

How to play

1. Split the players into two teams.

2. Place the chairs in two lines going down the room. Each team stands on the chairs in one of the lines.

3. Players then have to get all team members and chairs to the end of the room without getting off the chairs.

4. If a player cheats or falls off, the whole team goes back to the beginning and starts again.

63 Cup-balancing

What you need

- 1 jug of water per team
- 1 plastic cup per player
- 1 bucket per team
- 1 measuring jug

Age range

Juniors/secondary

How to play

1. Split the players into two teams.

2. Select one player from each team to hold the jug of water and to pour.

3. Team members take it in turns to run forward, lie on their back and place a plastic cup on their forehead.

4. The pourer must then fill the cup with water.

5. Players must then take the cup of water back to their team and empty it into their bucket.

6. This is repeated until each player has had a turn.

7. The winning team is the one with the most water in the bucket at the end.

Note: Be prepared for wet players and floors!

64 Alphabet scavenger hunt

What you need

- 1 plastic bag for each team

Age range

Juniors/secondary

How to play

1. Split players into teams of three or four.

2. Give each team a different letter of the alphabet.

3. Each team has ten minutes to collect as many things as possible from around the building that begin with that letter.

4. The winning team is the one with the most items.

65 Balloon defence

ㅐㅠㅐ

What you need

- 2 sets of different coloured balloons, approx. 25–50 for each team

Age range

Juniors/secondary

How to play

1. Split players into two teams.

2. Each team has a different colour set of balloons.

3. Each team must defend its treasure (the pile of balloons) while attempting to steal or destroy the other team's treasure.

4. The main aim is to steal all the other team's treasure without destroying the balloons.

5. Set a time limit on the game (I recommend 5–10 minutes).

6. When the time is up, each team's unstolen and undestroyed balloons count for 100 points each; any balloons they have taken from the other team are worth 200 points each.

66 Tug of war

What you need
- 1 length of strong rope
- A marker for the floor

Age range
Juniors/secondary

How to play
1. Divide the players into two teams.

2. Lay the rope on the ground. Place the marker on the ground half-way along.

3. Each team takes hold of half of the rope so that the two teams are facing each other.

4. The objective is to pull the other team past the central marker using as much strength as possible.

67 Get the keys

What you need

- 1 chair
- 1 bunch of keys
- 1 blindfold

Age range

Juniors/secondary

How to play

1. One player sits blindfolded on a chair in the middle of the room. Place the bunch of keys under the chair.

2. One at a time, other players come forward to try to retrieve the keys without being heard.

3. The player seated on the chair must listen out for the other player and point to where he or she thinks the other player is coming from. If correct, the person pointed to is out and the next player has a go.

The winner is the player who can retrieve the keys and return to his or her seat without being caught.

68 Mini-Olympics

What you need

- Blu-Tack or adhesive putty
- Rice
- Balloons
- Milk-bottle lids
- String
- Tables
- Chairs

Age range

Juniors/secondary

How to play

1. Divide the players into teams.

2. Team members must sign up for one or more of the following Olympics games and then compete against each other:

   Javelin: Throwing straws with Blu-Tack or adhesive putty on the end.
   Shotput: Throwing balloons filled with rice
   Discus: Throwing milk-bottle lids
   Wrestling: Arm wrestling
   Hammer throw: Throwing balloons filled with rice and with a piece of string tied round the end

Variation:
By adding other games, this can be set up as a whole Olympics evening.

69 Hunt the leader

What you need

- Clipboards
- Pens
- Willing leaders!

Age range

Secondary

How to play

1. Before the group arrives, leaders go into town or another designated area in disguise.

2. The group is then divided into teams (have a minimum of three or four people per team).

3. For safety, members of teams should stick together. It is a good idea to have a non-participating leader with each team.

4. The teams are sent off to find all their disguised leaders (this is not as easy as it sounds!).

5. When each team finds a leader, it must get that leader's signature (or even take a photo) as proof.

6. Each team must get as many signatures/photos as possible before the other teams get them.

7. Ideas for leaders' disguises: persuade a shopkeeper to let you 'help' behind the counter, dress as a tramp, old person, tourist, fireman, workman, etc. Some could dress up in obvious disguises, such as a lion or bear. Be as enterprising as possible.

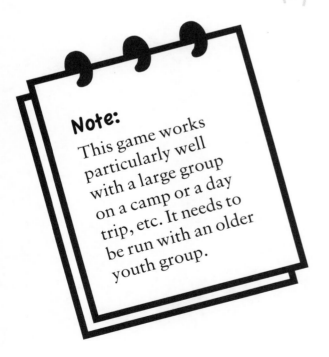

Note:
This game works particularly well with a large group on a camp or a day trip, etc. It needs to be run with an older youth group.

70 Sponge pick-up

What you need

• Lots of sponges

Age range

Secondary

How to play

1. Split the group into four teams.

2. Put one team in each corner of the room.

3. Drop all the sponges in the middle of the room.

4. If you call 'Three', each team must collect three sponges from the middle.

5. Only one player from each team may run to the pile and pick up a sponge. He or she places the sponge on the floor in front of the team, and the next player runs and collects, and so on.

6. The idea is to be the first team to collect the right number of sponges.

7. You can call larger numbers. If there are not enough sponges in the middle, teams can 'steal' from other teams, but only one player from each team may collect a sponge at a time, and team members may not touch other players or prevent them from taking a sponge from their pile.

71 Imagine

What you need

- Some common household items
- 1 table

Age range

Juniors/secondary

How to play

1. Put the household items on a table in front of you.

2. Each player comes up to you one at a time. Hand the players an object.

3. They must then act out something using that object, but without speaking (e.g. a hole punch can become a car accelerator pedal, a blanket can become Superman's cape, etc.).

4. Everyone else must guess what they are acting out.

72 I went on holiday and I took...

What you need

Age range

Juniors/secondary

How to play

1. The first player thinks of a word beginning with the letter 'a' and then says, for example, 'I went on holiday and I took an apricot.'

2. The next player repeats the sentence and adds something beginning with 'b'; for example, 'I went on holiday and I took an apricot and a balloon.'

3. The next player adds a word beginning with 'c': 'I went on holiday and I took an apricot, a balloon and a cake.'

4. The game continues until someone can't remember the list or makes a mistake. Depending on the person's age, you can either prompt or disqualify this player! Keep going until all players but one have been disqualified, or until you reach the end of the alphabet.

73 Photo shop

What you need

- Different and unconnected photos: enough for 5 per team

Age range

Juniors/secondary

How to play

1. Divide the players into teams. Give each team a set of five photos.

2. Each team then has to come up with a story that connects all five of its photos together.

74 Word association

What you need

- 1 small ball

Age range

Juniors/secondary

How to play

1. Everyone should be seated or standing in a circle.

2. The first player takes the ball and thinks of a word, e.g., 'milk'.

3. He or she then throws the ball to another player, saying 'Milk'.

4. That player must then throw the ball to someone else and say a word associated with milk, e.g., 'Cow'.

5. This then continues around the circle, ending up with word association a bit like this: Milk—Cow—Farm—Tractor—Combine harvester, etc.

75 How well do you know me?

What you need

- Paper and a pen for every player

Age range

Secondary

How to play

1. Everyone sits in a circle.

2. All players write down two things that are true and one thing that is not true about themselves.

3. Players take it in turns to read out their facts and the other players have to guess which one is not true.

76 Odd one out

What you need
- Sets of pictures, 1 set for each team; in each set, all of the pictures except one must be on a related theme

Age range
Secondary

How to play
1. Divide the players into teams.
2. Each team is given a set of pictures. Teams must work out which picture in their set is the odd one out.

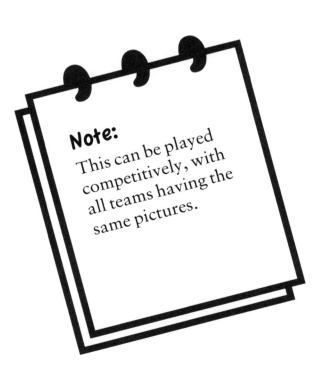

Note:
This can be played competitively, with all teams having the same pictures.

77 Story-telling

What you need

Age range

Secondary

How to play

1. Seat everyone in a circle.

2. Begin by telling the opening phrase in a made-up story. Then go round the circle, letting each player add a sentence or phrase to the story.

3. Here are a few story starters:

   Once I found a pot of gold and …
   One day my dog started to talk and …
   A giant knocked on my door and …
   I woke up one morning and I could fly …

Easy-going games

78 The chocolate game

What you need

- 1 large bar of chocolate (the game is harder if the chocolate comes straight out of the fridge)
- 1 plate
- 1 knife
- 1 fork
- Dice
- 1 hat
- 1 scarf
- 1 coat
- 1 pair of gloves

Age range

All ages

How to play

1. Seat everyone in a large circle.

2. Place all the clothes in the centre.

3. Put the chocolate (still in its wrapper) on the plate, with the knife and fork at its side, in the centre of the circle.

4. Players must take it in turns to roll the dice.

5. When a player rolls a six, he or she must put on all the clothes, pick up the knife and fork and try to eat the chocolate. This player keeps going until another player rolls a six.

6. The player in the centre must then hand over the clothes to the new player and rejoin the circle. This new player now dresses in all the clothes and tries to eat the chocolate.

7. The game finishes when all the chocolate has been eaten.

Note:
If you have lots of players, you may wish to have several games running simultaneously.

79 Guess that tune

What you need

- Pre-organized CD of short clips of well-know music (e.g., from TV theme tunes or current popular songs)

Age range

All ages

How to play

1. Play the group a clip from the CD.
2. Players have to guess what the tune is.

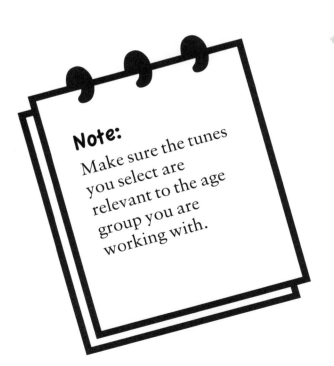

Note:
Make sure the tunes you select are relevant to the age group you are working with.

80 **Pictionary**

What you need
- Pens and paper

Age range
All ages

How to play
1. Divide the players into teams.

2. Each team appoints a player to come forward. Tell this player to draw a particular object.

3. That player must then return to the rest of his or her team and draw the picture. The player is not allowed to speak.

4. The first team to guess what the picture is gets the point.

81 Handbag game

What you need

Age range
All ages

How to play

1. Divide the players into teams.

2. Shout out an item. One player from each team must find the item from a team member's handbag and run to you with it.

3. Points are awarded to the first team that produces the item.

4. Items could include the following:

watch	shoelace
1-pence coin	earring
pen	trainer
credit card	wedding ring
1 tissue	keys
hair band	mobile phone
jumper	scarf
receipt	

Note:
This is good for a family games night, when there may be more women with bags.

82 Find someone who...

What you need

- Sheet listing about 20 categories—1 sheet per player (see sample opposite)
- Paper
- Pens

Age range

All ages

How to play

1. Give everyone a sheet listing the categories.

2. Each player must find someone whose name they can write down next to each category.

3. Players may only use each person once.

4. Players cannot write down the name of someone who isn't present.

5. Players cannot write their own name down under a category.

NAME ....

Find someone who ...

1. supports Manchester United football team ....
2. has a dog ....
3. likes Indian food ....
4. had cornflakes for breakfast ....
5. speaks French fluently ....
6. works for BT ....
7. likes ironing ....
8. is left-handed ....
9. plays tennis ....
10. has blue eyes ....
11. has been to the USA ....
12. can drive a car ....
13. can swim ....
14. wears a watch on the right wrist ....
15. is on Facebook ....
16. is wearing blue socks ....
17. has been on the London Eye ....
18. has won an award ....
19. didn't have turkey for Christmas lunch in 2008 ....
20. can play a musical instrument ....

83 Taste the crisps

What you need

- Lots of different-flavoured potato crisps (at least 6 different flavours)
- Bowls—1 for each flavour of crisps

Age range

All ages

How to play

1. Place a few crisps of each flavour in a bowl, each labelled with a number.

2. Players must taste the crisps in turn and write down what flavour they think they are.

Note:
Don't forget to make a note for yourself of which number corresponds to which crisp flavour.

84 Party Ring pass

What you need

- 1 packet of Fox's Party Ring biscuits or other ring-shaped snack
- 1 straw per player

Age ranges

All ages

How to play

1. Divide the players into teams.

2. All the players place the straws in their mouths.

3. The first team member hooks the Party Ring onto his or her straw. The Party Ring must be passed to every team member without using any hands and without dropping it.

85 Mummy!

What you need
- Lots of cheap toilet paper

Age range
All ages

How to play
1. Divide the players into teams.

2. One team member volunteers to be the 'mummy'.

3. The rest of the team must wrap this player up with the toilet paper so that he or she looks like an Egyptian mummy.

4. Points are awarded for speed, for the best mummy, for the fewest gaps in the wrapping, etc.

Christmas variation:
Provide hats, scarves, gloves, etc., and call them snowmen!

86 Orange relay

What you need

- 1 orange per team

Age range

All ages

How to play

1. Divide the players into teams.

2. The team members stand in a line, one behind the other.

3. The first player grips the orange beneath his or her chin without using hands.

4. The orange must pass down the line from player to player without any hands being used.

5. If the orange is dropped, it must go back to the beginning and the team must start again.

6. When the orange reaches the last person in the line, he or she runs to the front and starts passing it again.

7. When all the players are back in their original places, the team sits down.

8. The first team sitting down wins.

87 Beach art

What you need

Age range

All ages

How to play

1. Group the players into pairs.

2. Using whatever is on the beach, each pair has thirty minutes to make a work of art: a picture, model, etc.

3. The leaders judge which is the best picture at the end.

88 Jigsaws

What you need

- About 5 jigsaw puzzles per team (they must be of the same difficulty, if not the same jigsaws)

Age range

All ages

How to play

1. Divide the group into teams of about three players.

2. Each team has ten minutes to complete as many jigsaws as possible.

3. The team to complete the most in ten minutes wins.

89 Fruit bowl

What you need

• Chairs

Age range

Infants/juniors

How to play

1. All the players sit on chairs in a circle.

2. Choose three fruits and then name all the players one of those fruits.

3. Make one player stand in the centre of the circle and get rid of his or her chair.

4. That player calls out the name of a fruit. All the players with that name must then run to another chair as fast as possible, including the player who was in the centre.

5. The player left without a chair goes in the centre next.

6. If a player is in the circle more than three times, he or she is out. Players may not move to a seat directly next to their own.

90 Plate-spinner

What you need

- 1 plate

Age range

Juniors/secondary

How to play

1. Give all the players a number and sit them in a circle.

2. Spin the plate in the centre of the circle and call a number. The player with that number must catch the plate before it falls.

3. If the player succeeds, he or she gets to spin the plate and call another number; if the player fails to catch the plate before it falls, he or she must pay a forfeit (tell a joke, pull a face, sing a nursery rhyme, etc.).

91 Categories game

What you need

- 1 blank categories sheet per team (see sample sheet opposite)
- 1 pen per team

Age range

Juniors/secondary

How to play

1. Split the group into teams.

2. Give each team a pen and a categories worksheet.

3. Call out a letter of the alphabet.

4. The team must then complete the categories grid as fast as possible; each category must be filled in using a word beginning with the letter called out by the leader.

5. When a team has completed all the boxes, everyone in that team shouts 'STOP!' All teams must then stop filling in categories for that letter and move on to the next letter that is called out.

6. Repeat until the categories grids are completed.

7. Scoring: 1 point is given for every correct answer that no other team got; no points are given if another team has the same answer.

8. Categories can be varied depending on the theme.

Categories game worksheet

Letter	Food	Name	Chocolate bar	Country	Car make/model	Film

92 Pegs in hands

What you need
- Lots of pegs

Age range
Juniors/secondary

How to play
1. Put the players into pairs.

2. Using only one hand, one member from each pair has five minutes to get as many pegs as possible into his or her hand.

3. The other member of the pair can't help but counts the number held.

4. After five minutes, they swap roles.

5. The pair that together held the most pegs wins.

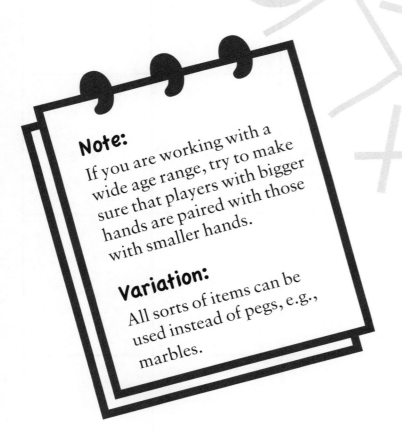

Note:
If you are working with a wide age range, try to make sure that players with bigger hands are paired with those with smaller hands.

Variation:
All sorts of items can be used instead of pegs, e.g., marbles.

93 Wink murder

What you need

Age range

Juniors/secondary

How to play

1. Get everyone to sit in a circle.

2. Send one player (the 'detective') out of the room.

3. While the detective is out of the room, choose one player in the group to be the 'murderer'.

4. Bring the detective back in and stand him or her in the centre of the circle.

5. The murderer must now 'kill' all the other players by winking at them.

6. The detective must guess who the murderer is before all the other players 'die'.

94 Book hold

What you need

- 2 heavy books
- Stop watch

Age range

Juniors/secondary

How to play

1. Split the group into two teams.

2. The first player from each team must hold out his or her arms; a book is then placed on each arm.

3. The players must hold out their arms for as long as possible.

4. Score as follows:

   5 points for 1 minute.
   10 points for 2 minutes.
   20 points for 3 minutes, etc.

5. Each team member has a go. All the scores are then combined and the team with the highest score wins.

95 Chubby bunnies

What you need

- Lots of marshmallows
- 1 bowl

Age range

Juniors/secondary

How to play

1. Get two volunteers. They have to fit as many marshmallows into their mouths as possible.

2. Make sure someone is counting the number as they put them in their mouths.

3. Have the bowl ready for them to spit out the marshmallows afterwards.

96 Human noughts and crosses

What you need

• 9 chairs

Age range

Juniors/secondary

How to play

1. Place the chairs in three rows of three.

2. Split players into two teams. Name one team 'noughts' and the other, 'crosses'.

3. Number the players in the teams.

4. Call out three numbers, e.g., 1, 4, 7. The players with these numbers on both teams run forward and have to try to complete the noughts and crosses board with their bodies as soon as possible while stopping the other team doing it first.

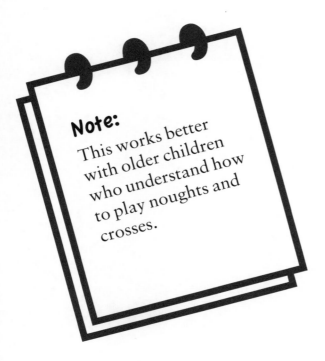

Note:
This works better with older children who understand how to play noughts and crosses.

97 Ball 1 to 2

What you need

- 1 ball
- 1 chair per player

Age range

Juniors/secondary

How to play

1. Split the players into two teams.

2. Seat them on chairs facing each other.

3. Number all the players on team 1 from left to right. Number all the players on team 2 from right to left.

4. One player takes the ball and throws it to a member of the opposite team saying, 'Number … [his or her own number] to number … [number of the other player].'

5. The other player must catch the ball and repeat the process.

6. If a player shouts a wrong number, drops the ball or throws to someone who is out, he or she is out.

7. Each team aims to get the opposite team out.

98 I pass you these scissors

What you need
- 1 pair of scissors

Age range
Juniors/secondary

How to play

1. Don't explain the rules of this game to the group.

2. Seat everyone in a circle.

3. Pass the scissors to the player sitting next to you. If your legs are crossed, then, while passing the scissors, you should say, 'I pass you these scissors crossed.' If your legs are uncrossed, you should say, 'I pass you these scissors uncrossed.'

4. The scissors themselves can be open or closed.

5. The next player then passes the scissors to the person next to him or her in the same way, and so on round the circle. It helps if you have a few other leaders sitting in the circle who know the rules.

6. It always takes a while for the players to work out why, for example, the scissors are sometimes open and yet it's correct to say 'uncrossed', etc.

7. Keep going until all the players catch on.

8. If some are finding it difficult to catch on, make exaggerated movements when crossing and uncrossing your legs.

99 Egg protectors

What you need

Each team needs:
- 1 egg
- 3 sheets of A3 or large paper
- String
- Sticky tape
- Materials for decoration, e.g., self-adhesive shapes, foam shapes, colouring pens, etc.

Age range

Juniors/secondary

How to play

1. Split the group into teams of three.

2. The idea is to build a package to protect but also display an egg, using the three sheets of paper, string and sticky tape.

3. Teams can decorate their packages.

4. When all the packages are ready, drop each team's egg in turn from the same height.

5. The team whose egg does not break wins.

100 Bunyippa

What you need

Age range

Secondary

How to play

1. Split the group into two teams and line the teams up so that they are facing each other.

2. Two players, one from each team and from opposite ends of the lines, move forward to face each other.

3. They then fix eyes on each other and shout 'Bunyippa click!'

4. Thy then each have to move to the opposite end of the room without breaking eye contact with their opponent.

5. The other players on the sidelines may do anything to distract the player from the opposite team, but at no point must there be any physical contact. A player from the sidelines may not move into the path of the opposing team's player.

6. If one of the two main players breaks eye contact or laughs, he or she is captured and joins the other team.

7. The winning team is the one with the most members once all have had a go.

101 Table-top challenge

What you need

- 10 table-top games, e.g., Connect Four, Jenga, etc.
- 10 tables

Age range

Secondary

How to play

1. Place the tables in a circle and set out the games, one on each table. Give a score card to each player.

2. Allow players five minutes to play each game.

3. At the end of five minutes, one player from each table must move clockwise to the next table; the other player must move anticlockwise to a different table.

4. In this way, each player should challenge someone different for each game.

5. Players must note the number of points they get for each game on their score cards.

Note:
You will need to adjust these guidelines according to the number of players in your group.

Index

Also available

How to run children's clubs and meetings

Practical suggestions for
people in youth ministry

STEVEN WALKER

144PP, PAPERBACK

ISBN 978-1-84625-060-6

We would love to see people appear out of the
blue who are superbly gifted at working with
children and teenagers. These workers would
have unlimited energy and patience, and be
highly organized so that everything ran with
barely a hitch.

Unfortunately, people like this are extremely
rare. Perhaps you wonder whether you have
what it takes to help with children's clubs.
Maybe you already help with a children's club
or meeting, but often feel that you are simply
muddling along. You may have been helping
with children's clubs for a number of years.
Whatever your involvement in children's
work, this Bible-based yet thoroughly practical
book is designed to help you, as Steven Walker
uses his considerable experience to provide
encouragement as well as ideas and guidelines
for all who assist with this ministry.

*'...an attractive resource for all
those who want to impact young
lives to the glory of God.'*

**—J. Phil Arthur, Pastor, Free Grace
Baptist Church, Lancaster, United
Kingdom**

ABOUT DAY ONE:

Day One's threefold commitment:

- To be faithful to the Bible, God's inerrant, infallible Word;
- To be relevant to our modern generation;
- To be excellent in our publication standards.

I continue to be thankful for the publications of Day One. They are biblical; they have sound theology; and they are relevant to the issues at hand. The material is condensed and manageable while, at the same time, being complete—a challenging balance to find. We are happy in our ministry to make use of these excellent publications.

JOHN MACARTHUR, PASTOR-TEACHER, GRACE COMMUNITY CHURCH, CALIFORNIA

It is a great encouragement to see Day One making such excellent progress. Their publications are always biblical, accessible and attractively produced, with no compromise on quality. Long may their progress continue and increase!

JOHN BLANCHARD, AUTHOR, EVANGELIST AND APOLOGIST

Visit our web site for more information and to request a free catalogue of our books.

www.dayone.co.uk

U.S. web site:

www.dayonebookstore.com